Kim,
Thank you for your sweet, sweet spirit thank you. Your love & support willingness of Kingdom. I appreciate you
Shaniequa

MW00712438

Leading From The Front

Shaniequa L. Washington

Leading From The Front

Publisher:
Shaniequa L. Washington
Beaufort, South Carolina

Copyright ©2015 Shaniequa L. Washington.

All Rights Reserved. No part of this publication may be reproduced, stored in a retrieval system. No part of this publication is to be transmitted in any form or by any means, electronic, mechanical, photocopying, recording or otherwise, without the written permission of the publisher.

Limits of Liability-Disclaimer

The author and publisher shall not be liable for your misuse of this material. The purpose of this book is to educate and entertain. The author and/or publisher do not guarantee that anyone following these techniques, suggestions, tips, ideas, or strategies will become successful. The author and/or publisher shall have neither liability nor responsibility to anyone with respect to any loss of damage caused, or alleged to be caused, directly or indirectly by the information contained in this book.

Unless otherwise specified, all scripture has been taken from the New King James version ©1982 by Thomas Nelson. All rights reserved.

Editing: Robin Devonish, The Self-Publishing Maven

Cover Design: Dynasty Barfield

Layout Design: Joy Turner, JetSet Communications & Consulting

ISBN-13: 978-0692507285

ISBN-10: 0692507280

Printed in the United States of America

"10% of life is what happened to you and 90% how I react to it."

Preface

Leadership is something that was absent in my life as a child. I grew up in the Bronx, New York in a place called Parkchester. Now this was to be considered the better part of the city, suburbia, a way of escape but please understand that destruction was still all around me.

I remember growing up and always being in a place where I was repeatedly told to do the right thing, but never shown or saw an example of the right thing to do. The elders within my family said we don't have dummies in our family, so go to school and get good grades. I never saw what success in school looked like, so just passing was good enough to me.

I was told to work hard but never taught how to grow and soar. I felt as long as I had a job and was being productive; this was good.

My elders drilled and said that I had to save money because you never know when you will have a rainy day. Well, it surely rained on us many times. It felt like we were going through a hurricane, and I never was able to see truly how the storm was beneficial. I thought it was normal to live from paycheck to paycheck and sometimes just barely making it. All of what I learned allowed me to see that what was in the front of me contradicted what I heard behind me.

Growing up, I did not have many role models or people to connect regularly with or shadow for learning. There was none for me to say; when I grow up I want to be just like her or him.

This lack was the beginning of the void. I remember a time while growing up; I experienced both sides of what life had to offer at that those particular times. One part club life and the other spiritual life, because, I had no example of anyone to lead me spiritually, I chose to party, hang out and do what I saw everyone do. And, I followed their specific instructions and became a professional in the party industry. I knew any everything that happened surrounding that life.

In my spiritual life, I went to church but my instructions were to sit in the pew and act appropriately. What was appropriate? Everything I saw and felt was rooted in judgment and condemnation, which did not lead me closer to Christ. I couldn't understand anything the Pastor said and all I knew were the repetitive scriptures the seniors of the church would use, along with, saying you were going to Hell. Well, let's just say I checked the hell box because there were no moral principles established for the kingdom of precepts being taught. The world ensured not only to give a key to the city but made sure to unlock the gate.

I felt empowered in the club and streets arena because I was welcomed, admired, and I was opening whatever door I felt like. In this arena, I led well because this society taught me how to expose myself for all to see, and this is where I believed "The Empire" was in the stuff. I thought that success was in how many Louis

Vuitton, Gucci and Coach Bags a person had. The material things meant you were the hottest chick on the block. But, then I grew up!

I found out, the doors I usually could open were now being slammed in my face. Where I once was admired, now, I was seen as being foolish, immature and having no sense of direction or fulfillment for my life. I felt like I was being led astray and was at a place of ground zero seeking to start all again. As I grew, I saw that social status only applied in certain arenas and mattered in the world of corporate foundation. It was not by what you had but to who were you connected. I found out quickly what I considered (club scene, ghetto life) as a view of success was the view of being a statistic and having no value.

While further reflecting, I thought to myself, where are the leaders? I love my mom and the place where we are today, her life today shows as a true example of redemption and God healing. However, at the time in my life, I needed her there. There were so many things I was going through, but she could not push me through because she was not able to push herself through her circumstances. She was in a dark place in her life where substance abuse led her and caused her to be in a place of blindness. Even if she wanted to see, she couldn't get out because her example of leading would only lead me to a road called destruction. The result was me to seeing another path of mystery causing me to feel confused and lost in a place of not knowing where to go and what I was supposed to do.

I thought, maybe I am supposed to find someone to take care of me, so, I got into a relationship with a millionaire who had all the luxurious life had to offer. We shopped, shopped and shopped and I had the finest of everything. I lived in a nice place with luxury furniture and never wanted for anything but craved love. I only was his trophy piece of "Beauty" to show that he had a banging girl on his arm. The so-called relationship resulted in abuse and being caged like in solitary confinement. He only wanted me to come out when he could keep tabs on me. He even isolated me from family, and I then feared the world I once knew very well. The behavior ultimately led to feelings of rejection. I found myself disconnected from places and people but connected to feelings of judgment and fear. I was concerned about being looked at through a scrutinized eye from the church, as well as, being rejected in my social status. The love that I thought was part of the plan now had become my bondage.

I thought why me and why was I being forsaken, not knowing, that God had a plan already designed for my life, and all I had to do was follow the path.

There was a breaking point as I look back at the details of my life. In small increments God was building, God was taking all of the hurt, disappointment and shame to mold me into greatness. He shaped trust, instilled integrity and from all I went through each and every situation built more character.

Where God was taking me, I just could not identify with it, and it all started with my childhood. If I did not experience the lack of being led I would not have desired to be the best leader and seek for the best leadership. My experiences began my journey of leading from the front. In this book, you get "one point for talking about it and nine points for execution". That's when you become the perfect ten! It is easy to say you're a leader, but you must realize that you first must be led. You can never take someone to a place where you have never been. I have been to a place called isolation, rejection, physical and emotional abuse, suicide, poverty, insecure, and a place called give up! All so I could "Lead from the front!"

Introduction

Leadership is the action of leading a group of people or an organization. According to God's Word, leadership is for all of us. It is an attitude, behavior, and influence. Each one of us needs to exhibit leadership qualities in our relationships with others, in our marriages, in our workplaces, in our child rearing, and in every other aspect of our lives.

In today's world, our country is losing its moral compass and there is an increased blurring line between what is right and what is wrong. In fact, varying definitions of right and wrong have been created, and the Bible provides the much needed moral compass.

My growth in leadership always started with me. I had to identify, embrace, and constantly change to grow. I learned from those who led me, learned from those things that did not work, those things that had a monumental influence over me.

I truly believe that to be a good leader, you first must be a good follower. I live to follow God as my first and ultimate leader and to honor and follow the leaders; he has placed in my life naturally and the spiritually. I would always hear the cliché growing up, "Be a leader and not a follower". It never really impacted until I understood what leadership meant.

My personal definition of leadership means, steering or directing with integrity, passion, purpose, and managing personally. A "Boss will say, "GO!" A leader will say, "Let's Go." This book is designed to illustrate the importance of effective leadership in the world that seems to be unled.

Never discount the purpose of your life and the course that it has to take to cultivate the shape of your destiny. There is always a plan for your life. God has declared that He is the Alpha and the Omega, and we will walk the middle, as only He knows the beginning and the end. Receive the glimpse and seek the path while you walk this thing out!

Jeremiah 1:5-"Before I have formed you in the womb I knew you, and before you were born I consecrated you; I appointed you a prophet to the nations."

Acknowledgements

During this process, several people covered me in prayer and were a blessing in my life. There were several encounters of relationships that caused a birthing and impartations of "Destiny" to come forth.

I want first to thank God for choosing me well before I accepted the greatness that he created in me.

I want to thank my wonderful husband, my covering who never doubted who I was and the ability that God has given me. "I love you Corey and I am forever yours!"

My four wonderful daughters who always support, stand by my side. My pep squad Kori, Bre'zhee, Ajanae, and Kiara mommy loves you more than words will ever express, this is a gift to say that there is nothing too hard for God.

I want to thank my wonderful Mother Odessa Jackson, who carried me for nine months and brought me from her womb into this world. My prayer is that my footsteps would be the definition of a great mother. I thank you for all that you have done in my life even in the times of struggle, as the struggles created a spirit of perseverance and wisdom.

Grandma Gloria wow oh wow, the wisdom, the pep talks and the many outpours of you reminding me to continue to pray, continue to cover and always remember to love. Grandma, you will always say, "love in spite of!"

I thank my spiritual parents Randy and Theresa Roberts; I thank you for your wisdom, your unconditional love and your trust in believing in who God created me to be.

I want to thank all those that I worked with who trusted me, believed in me and helped to mold me into greatness. Jim Torgerson, one of the best supervisors to ever work for and who teaches you to "Strive for Excellence Always!" Fredericka Howard, Mary Ellen Zander, Grey Ley and Nicole Rana, each one of you gave me something that kept on giving and now I have the ability to give this to someone else. I want to thank those who ever encouraged me, supported me and believed that saw greater, and never gave up on me!

Contents

Contents

Chapter One

Leadership and Why It is Important

Leadership plays a vital role in the success of many large corporations. In small organization's, leadership is important for personal growth. You have to lead yourself before you can inspire others to follow. Leaders are not just born. They are ordinary people, just like you and me, whose development came through shaping and influence. Leadership training and development can maximize productivity, shape positive characteristics, and promote harmony in environments. To achieve this, key people must lead individuals and teams using appropriate leadership styles. In this growth process of being molded into a leader, you must be willing to invest, invest in yourself. It is highly encouraged to take leadership development classes and to find someone who is sharper than you to sharpen you into the best leader you can be.

Leadership is never easy. No matter how effortless some leaders appear to manage, it is filled with constant obstacles, challenges, changes and surprises. However, it is not the leader's responsibility to solve every problem that arises. Great leaders empower and teach those they lead to take ownership identifying issues at the root and implement changes. Good leaders recognize that they do not have all of the answers and are constantly educating themselves and sharpening their tools and skills. Leaders are great communicators and ensure that they operate in a state of inclusion. They empower those who are connected to feel a part and those who are not, they work to ensure they will more likely become a part. In the process of communication, it is vital to understand what works for each and find the best course of communication. Never place all of your eggs in one basket.

Leadership and operating in purpose plays such a vital role in our world. We must be careful not to make the common mistake of placing ourselves on a platform, overestimating ourselves, or thinking we can't learn from those we lead. In fact, if you are presently in leadership, your team will learn from you if, you're humble, you will in turn, learn great aspects from your team.

Leadership is required to establish the generations ahead, in this current era it is evident to see that there is a lack of respect and honor for any person that has been established to teach or lead. The lack of respect and honor opens a portal for future generations to fail to lead.

In the Kingdom of God, there is a great void of leadership that operates according to the principles of God, and you can see this void from the pulpit to the pew. There is no respect for the house of God and to His word. Tradition and religious mentality have allowed Biblical principles to become watered down to fit each person's situation giving no charge to living the word as it is written.

Where are the leaders in the church in a position of no compromise, raising a standard of what scripture identifies leaders are to look like and how leaders are to carry themselves? In this day and age, there is a disconnect between Biblical and world teachings on how to be a true effective leader. In the world, it is every man for themselves and not investment or adding value to anyone else's life but their own. In Biblical leadership, it is never about you but about giving back, taking care of Gods people. In the kingdom, it is about one who creates a legacy to do greater than our forefathers did and established moral ethics and conduct that is pleasing to God.

As I continue to learn from great leaders in the professional arena and Spiritual arena's, I've been taught how to operate from a position of honor and integrity while positioning myself to grow and lead. A statement was given to me, and that has stuck with me from the time I heard it is, "If you protect your character, God will protect your reputation". The statement means you must lead with your character intact and allow nothing or no one to cause you to operate in placing your integrity on a bookshelf. You will not be able to restore that which your reputation has flawed!

In leading, I remember a time I worked for someone who did not have respect for women. He would say things that were disrespectful and cause you to operate in a state of offense on a daily basis. I had subordinates who would report to me and complain of his disrespect and how he would publicly embarrass and belittle them on purpose. This behavior showed most in front of other men and caused the women to have low self-worth and not want to work for him. I too felt this way, however, understood my role in leading and could not allow the impacts of what I was going through to be transparent and influence people to compromise their character. The people who worked there looked at me to lead the way.

I recall having a meeting with him to address his behavior not being of moral character and that I had enough respect for him to come personally and speak to him about it. However, he was warned that from that point on that if he continued with the behavior, I would report him. I made it clear that I was there to do my job well and did not want any unnecessary personality barriers and issues to be in the way.

I will never forget his response, "little girl don't worry about barriers because it took me five years to get where I am so don't look to go anywhere anytime soon". The response infuriated me and to be honest I wanted to go off! However, understanding that if I chose to go off I would have placed my integrity and character on a shelf. The reaction to his response was not worth it, so I calmed myself and led from the front with respect. I ensured that I was specific about what I did and strategic in how I managed the team. I made sure I was always a step ahead of him and when he tried to call me out on something I was already on it. I did not know this was only setting me up to be acknowledged, as a leader, in the eyes of the people. I was not thinking about being seen as an example, I was only thinking let me prove to this fool that you don't know what I'm made of. I will not allow a tyrant like you to stop me. My example led to promotion and not realizing that those who were watching were also promoted behind me not long after. My team shared with me that, during this challenge, I showed perseverance and streamed upwards in the face of adversity. The message within this portion of the book is, there are times where the odds are stacked so high that it seems impossible to climb the wall or knock it down. You must never doubt what you're strength, especially if you are operating in what you were called to do.

When I think of a scriptural teaching and the importance of leadership, the book of Judges comes to mind. There wasn't one qualified person in the entire city that could lead as a king. Because of this fact, Deborah, who stood on integrity and standards according to God's word, became the judge.

When you look at our world today, many ministries are trying to move forward in outreach and kingdom building but there is a severe void in leaders with integrity. This void lacks the ability to foster the characteristics of those who led them and put God first as the ultimate leader. God ordains leadership, and we have fallen from the principles as God has established them. Romans 13:1 reads "Let every person be subject to the governing authority for there is no authority except God, and those that exist have been instituted by God."

Leadership is important even if it means only leading yourself daily, towards God and God leading you into a place of righteousness. Invest at least 50 percent of your time in leading yourself into the right place, right purpose, and right method.

Leadership is about accountability and does not mirror the following:

➢ Control

➢ Micro-Management

Reflections:

> Do you feel that you have to micro-manage everything?

> Do you build trust in co-workers?

> Is there inclusion of those that you lead or dictatorship?

Chapter Two
My Attitude and What It Means

In leadership, your character normally is a key definition of your attitude. Your attitude, and how it's perception by those you are interacting with, determines the response received from what is being asked or targeted as a goal and the outcome.

Attitude means someone's opinions or feelings about something, especially shown by their behavior. Attitude reflects leadership. It is important for the one that is leading, even when dealing with the stress of execution and operating in excellence, never to lead while feeling frustration and impatience. It is easy to be a good leader when all is well, and the sun is bright. But how do you lead when the decks are stacked and about to fall over, the skies are cloudy, just about black on some days? When this happens, leadership matters the most. Note that, people under your leadership determine the type of person you are from your attitude.

The perception of an event will sometimes influence the reality of it. I want to share an experience in which I learned that your attitude and response means everything.

I recall when my mom became sober and cleaned up her life; I didn't have a good attitude towards her. I always reminded her of how she failed me, ensured she knew what she missed in my life and how she owed me. I made her feel as if she was subject to my torture because of what took place in the past. I didn't show an attitude of forgiveness or compassion but wanted forgiveness for everything I had done or said. It was a flaw in my character because my attitude toward her came with conditions. I did not want my flaw to be measured, but I had summed up everything she had done and charged her with high interest for it. My behavior did not show an attitude of love, but one of hatred and resentment.

This behavior did not represent the character that I was leading from in other areas of my life, which was, seeking the best and aiming high in greatness. I had to overcome and respond differently! The perception of how I was leading the relationship with my mom was one of disrespect, dishonor, hurt, and not knowing how to move on. My attitude made the difference!

In a previous sentence, I spoke about perception and people's reaction to your attitude. My now 20-year-old daughter grew up watching my attitude of disrespect and dishonor towards my mom. For a season, our relationship took a turn where she began to dishonor me. I began to ask why was this happening to me why was my daughter acting this way when I give her everything? I love her and make sure she never had to face the issues I grew up with, only to realize her response was from my attitude and what I displayed or did not display in leadership.

Growing up, my grandmother Gloria would always talk to me about my attitude and say it's not your place to cast or judge but to love and forgive. It was not until I accepted that my past had passed, and it was up to me in how I responded to it was the only way to change my attitude.

In leading, we must realize that our attitude is always being measured. We often have to step back and remind ourselves that the challenges we are going through are temporary, and it only becomes permanent when we decide to stay in that place. The lesson is, be careful that you don't "co-sign" your trial and stay in a place longer than intended because of a poor attitude. Another way to get an attitude adjustment is to stay connected to your God-given purpose. Knowing your purpose and what is required will prepare you to embrace the ride and become the encourager to those you lead. A great attitude shows great courage, trust, and belief in what you do. If your attitude reflects rude, people will be rude; disrespect, people will disrespect, unforgiveness, people will not forgive; quitter, your people will quit long before you have released that you have quit!

Scripture teaches us that the taller the order, the more you have to give. That is more patience, more time, more that you have to pour in to get out what you seek.

Luke 12:48 – "But the one who did not know, and did what deserved a beating, will receive a light beating. Everyone to whom much was given, of him, will be required, and from him to whom they entrusted much, they will demand more."

As a leader, you are entrusted with certain things and as you entrust there is a great requirement of your faithfulness to maintain this trust. Faithfulness requires that we manage things (attitude) wisely and unselfishly. Our attitude must have balance in all areas of our life, should show gratitude and empower those who operate via our leadership to move in the same strides and grace. Scripture speaks to those who murmur and complain.

Philippians 2:14 says "Do all things without murmuring and disputing."

As a leader, if you are always complaining and dissatisfied, you can never find good in any point of purpose, there is a problem. We have all been around those leaders who led well - they may have been tough; demanded a lot, but were fair, firm and consistent; and led with integrity character and charisma.

Who were those leaders that had a great attitude and impacted you?

Reflections:

➤ What is the most memorable moment that you can recall from those that impacted your life?

➤ What impact does a leader have on how you respond and produce?

> ➤ What are those things that caused you to walk away from purpose and dreams because of the interactions you have had with those leaders?

> ➤ How will you revitalize your dream, reposition your attitude, and move into not just leadership but being a great leader in leadership?

Think of some things people have shared with you about your personal attitude that do not reflect one of leadership according to the word, way, and will of God. Record those things in the space provided and give them to God!

_____

_____

_____

_____

_____

_____

_____

_____

_____

_____

_____

_____

_____

_____

_____

To close this chapter, Seek God with this prayer:

Lord this is _____ I come to you seeking help and healing from any attitudes that do not align with you. Forgive me Father for my trespasses against others and restore in me the spirit of you. As these past attitudes arise, I pray that the Holy Spirit will guide me to a place of new. I declare a new attitude and new language, in Jesus' Name. Amen.

Chapter Three
Behavior Matters

B ehavior is a portion of you that carries weight and determines how people respond to you. Your personal behavior gives a portrait of your morals and personal beliefs, your level of respect and integrity. As a leader, your personal behavior is measured by your interactions. Understand that when your behavior does not measure to what you present it to be, it is often viewed as the cliché, "Do as I say, but not as I do". Leading from a behavior of, I have earned that right, and not of I will always do what's right. I will never ask you to do what I am not willing to do. Your behavior determines how many people will follow and embrace the vision of what has been established or in manifestation before them.

Many successful leaders model great behavior and find the balance between personal and business. When there is a mix, instead of the balance of business and personal, there is a conflict that influences bad behavior and causes making of bad decisions. The poor behavior creates inconsistency in leadership and causes people to follow suit or trends that die quickly or come on strong. The results of poor behavior may also create ripples and unsettled damage, which will redirect the path of a person who once was dedicated and fully vested to becoming unengaged and no longer interested. In most times, you will see a huge decline in performance and a shift in that person's overall attitude.

Your personal behavior is your attitude, communication patterns, informal team processes, personality and the conflicts of it, political behavior, competency, and skills. How do you react when people react and/or do not react to what you believe? What do you want and say, as you remind yourself that unspoken behavior brings undetermined perceptions leaving one always to wonder about the individual who stands before them and calls themselves a leader? I want to share with you how learning the right behaviors when growing and leading can determine the outcome.

In leading, I have had the privilege of being connected and meeting tons of people. Sometimes in those settings people believe they can determine the response or the actions of your behavior because of what everyone else is doing.

I was in an environment simply grabbing a bite to eat, and we were in a large group. Everyone ordered off of the menu, and things seemed to be going well; there was small talk taking place at the table with laughter back and forth. The food came out and oh my goodness!

Immediately, one individual complained before the plate could get on the table stated, "this is wrong! I could see it is wrong this is not what I asked for! Take this back I am not paying for this."

The next individual jumped on the bandwagon and began to shout, "my food is cold what were you doing holding the food so that it came out at the same time? Excuse me, you knew this was a large table I want the manager!"

Well, the manager comes out and needless to say discounted the food. I was appalled at what I saw next. Everyone who attacked this poor waiter and complained to the manager, before you knew it, either paid a fraction or nothing at all. I can assure you they all ate as if they paid for what they got. The waiter comes to me and says, "ma'am, I am so sorry about the food, how is your meal?" I answered, "I apologize for the mix-up. Sir, thank you for asking and my food is fine."

You may wonder what does this have to do with anything at all. Well, the following week I was at work, and someone came up to me and said, "I don't know how you handled being with those horrible people. I saw you as I was in the booth in the corner across from you. That was a nightmare how those people were so rude and nasty to the waiter to get free food. The things that people would do in this world." The next question that came to me from that individual was, "do you go out with them a lot?"

What if my behavior was poor or my attitude was not up to par, we never know who is watching and what will be the response based on what they see or hear?

The Bible speaks of leadership and our behaviors. Hebrews 13:7 reads, "Remember them which have the rule over you, who have spoken unto you the word of God: whose faith follow considering the end of their conversation."

We must be careful with our behavior that we're not adopting other people attitudes and behaviors. One story that truly illustrates the consequences of bad behavior and operating out of world's systems is of Samson in Judges, chapters 13 through 16. Samson lived a life of greed, and he loved the world. Samson's desire to love the world controlled his life (living for other people). Samson spent his time fulfilling the pleasures of his flesh, and he believed that nobody could overcome him.

Have you ever worked with or for someone who felt that they were irreplaceable?

Sampson soon found out he was replaceable. The book of Judges is a sad record, but a revealing truth of how important one's behavior is. It revealed people's greed for material things much like the world we live in today. In that era, people were proud and trusted in only themselves, much like the people of today and the leadership that prevails. As you read along in Judges, there is a sign of relief when the Jews return to God for help. With today's economic state in such turmoil and as world systems have become dominant over values, we must return to God. There are a series of stories in Judges that all follow the same pattern of sin. Because of the behavior choices, there is a suffering and punishment. Those stories align with what we see today through choices of drugs, alcohol, greed, and corruption that creates a world system of self and personal gain leaving leaders to direct people to a place of self-destruction. The leaders illustrated in Judges were ineffective as they failed to find God in their lives.

This example gives reflection to why God has inspired me to share the importance of being a leader. Not just any leader, but one who is accountable to God and chooses to live a life without compromise. We have to know the signs of our behaviors and seek God for right determination and ask in honesty, "Are we the leaders He called and ordained us to be?" We must open ourselves to the spirit of truth as we ask the questions:

➢ Do we want things to please ourselves?

➢ Do we want things we see that others have? Is there manipulation in how you lead people or control situations for our sake?

➢ Do we discount the gifts and talents of others that God has provided as provision for our vision?

Let's see the direct cause of Samson's failure:

> Samson failed to obey Gods word! Is your behavior one of disobedience to God? Do you rebel against God or those who lead you?

> He did not love God's people! Do you feel that you can do this alone and disrespect those that have been divinely appointed to be a part of your life? Be wise. Those who stand in agreement with the cliché, "I can do bad all by myself", surely can!

> Samson failed to give honor to God! Do you realize, accept, and operate in knowing that you can do all things through Christ that strengthens you and are nothing without Him?

As leaders, we must recognize our behavior before we can lead someone in theirs. We must know to whom we belong and operate in what

He has ordained and established. God's attitude should be ours - one of integrity, love, forgiveness, and hope. As a leader, we should lead the hopeless to a place of hope and those lost to a place of found. We should lead the blind to a place of sight and the deaf to a place so of hearing. A boss says, "GO!" Leaders say, "Let's go!"

Reflections:

> ➢ Do you allow the course of what is takes place in the world determine how you interact and respond as a leader in the workplace?

> ➢ Do you feel that to be a successful leader you have to compromise your faith and beliefs?

> ➢ How will you seek to change to become the ordained leader as God established?

Chapter Four
The Power of Influence

Influence is "the act or power of producing an effect without apparent exertion of force or direct exercise of command and emanation of spiritual or moral force. The corrupt interference with authority for personal gain; the power or capacity of causing an effect in indirect or intangible ways."

Where do you stand after reading all of these definitions of influence? Influence, if used morally, would be impactful in cultivating and rearing a culture to powerful leadership. When you reflect back on the events that happened in your lifetime, it is the course of positive or negative experiences that inspired change, or perhaps influenced an attitude not to change. As I recall and reflect back on my life, it was the things that were the hardest in my life that impacted me the most. The hard things influenced me to do something different to produce a different result. I did not like the facts before me, so I decided to change them and create history. I learned that you must choose to do something contrary to status quo.

Influence can be for good or evil, but as a leader the desire should be to influence one to greatness beyond the measure of what's already produced. When I think of the pyramid of influence, I think of what it takes to gain results when operating in integrity and doing things earnestly. The pyramid starts with empowerment. You must choose to be powerful. People can speak that you are, or can be a powerful leader, but unless you decide to operate in that power, it is merely a vision.

As I reflect on the meaning of the word power, I think of what is needed to influence. What surrounds that word would be vision (most visionaries possess power) and persuasion (influence means how do I get the people to…). Operating in power constantly promotes positive reinforcement. We sometimes have to remind those who become discouraged of what their purpose is when it does not look like purpose. There is a time in leadership where discipline is necessary, and chastisement is needed to create an atmosphere of integrity and moral character. Discipline creates an influence of consistency, faithfulness, and expertise. A wise man, Pastor Randy Roberts, once said, "Never take advice from one you are not willing to trade places with." Such powerful words are from a great leader (influencer) who has inspired my life.

I can remember the first time I felt like I was inspired, there was something released into my life was when I worked for a lady named Nicole Rana, who gracefully took me under her wing. I would always see her doing important things and would ask what are you doing, and she would share the task and ask do you want to know how to do it and show me. I began to gain confidence in what I saw and experienced, and it increased my level of trust for her. One day Nicole called me in her office to gain understanding of my career goals. At the time, I was fine with where I was but Nicole reminded me that I deserved more and should never stop aiming for better. I found it cool but still not convinced this would be right for me or that I would even have the ability to have access to this.

A couple of weeks later Nicole and I were having another discussion about success and career paths, and she asked if I wanted to go to the year beginning meeting at the company we both worked. I always thought this was huge as all of the executives, movers and shakers are there. The experience was unforgettable as I was able to stand in the presence of the elite and partake in executive conversations. This experience was the fire that made me move! In the following two weeks our team bonused, and I was all very happy with my bonus. Who doesn't need extra money? Hooray! Nicole and I were talking, I shared with her the fact that I was happy we received our bonus and what I planned to do. She showed me her check, and I almost fainted! At that moment I said, there is a door of access that I'm not walking through. Nicole continued to keep me under her wing, would always give me those great pep talks, Nicole showed me how to do many things and the best route for getting things done. I am today forever grateful to her, as she taught me how to be a great leader (influencer) you have to have the will to follow. We know the hold saying, you can take the horse to the water, but you can't make them drink it. The many talks of finances, character, being mindful of the company you keep and your interactions with people, networking. These are things I did not see growing up, and if Nicole did not see what she saw within me to influence, I don't know where I would be. I do know I thank God that this was part of His blueprint, as it was a game changer.

We must be in contact with those who know what is going on. In the Bible, God illustrates the power of influence with Israel, a chosen people, surrounded by many that worshiped idol gods.

God wanted His people of Israel to be holy. When we as leaders move into the power of influence, our first influence must be God. We must choose to worship God and God alone no matter what! This practice will mature us, build character, and bring us to a place of cautiousness. The reverence and fear of God will lead us to make right decisions, decisions that can impact all that is connected to us. God establishes in Deuteronomy 13:6 that Israel is to fear Him and not allow wickedness to continue in the land.

You may be asking what this means for you. The power of influence is too strong to ignore. With our influence, we must lead from the front, understand our call, and say "yes" to our purpose. Our influence will be the life that we live which inspires others to obtain greatness through integrity, perseverance, and willingness to do great exploits for God.

The Bible declares that we are living in end times, leaders must take a stand and pour into the next generation. We must inspire and know that the measure of success is not how naked can you be, how many cars you own, or how many reality shows you make it on. Those influences are simply wrong and seek to enslave the mind.

As leaders, and those who desire to lead, we must understand the accountability to those who we are appointed to us. We must end the wicked influences in the land and realize that the generation being raised has become crafty and swift at turning the word to fit their situation. These beliefs only lead to imparting polluted doctrine.

Leaders of influence are required to stand, watch and protect the virtue of those we are appointed over even when they do not realize it needs to be protected. James 1:5 clearly states "if any of you lacks wisdom, let him ask of God, who gives to all liberally and without reproach, and it will be given to him."

Influence was a major part of God's working in the New Testament. The Apostle Paul set forth an example to be noted and followed. It is only the power of God within and the grace of God at work bringing influences to bear upon us. Who are those leaders previously appointed in your life that has had great influence? Who are those leaders and teachers that cause a humbleness in your spirit where you constantly thank God for all that He has done and t has been imparted to cause great change for the better in your life? Reflect on the times when you felt you were in a "no way out" situation and temptation was determined to be your influence. As you began to seek the Lord, that thing turned itself around. The word declares that God will give you the ability to endure the temptation and give you a way of escape. It would be the words communicated and the teachings that dwell within you that cause you to rise above the temptation purposed to influence you into a place of self-destruction.

"Influence" is very powerful as it can lead a generation to a place of purpose or a place of pain. Influence can help one emulate greatness, success, righteousness, purpose, victory, happiness, joy, and contentment. These are all places you have to decide to go even though you may not know how to get there. Often we have a great desire to do better than before, to do greater than our previous generation did. The one thing that stands between our great desire and that success is the "how" when our will says "yes." This action is when the one that has been appointed to lead must recognize the will of an individual and impart the how. Then the seed is planted which helps the desire to grow and move past a dream into a reality.

Many people often think success comes easy. Well, it does not always come easy, but when it comes all of the things that molded you to that place now becomes tools for success. Those tools can influence someone with an empty tool box to begin using the tools you've learned.

Under the influence of great leadership, one must use the tools to chisel away the barrier of adversity and molded into a place called growth and maturity, ending up in a place called success. It does not matter if you are a School Teacher,

CEO, Pastor or Evangelist. You can be a Mentor, Sister, Brother, Mother, Father, Friend, Aunt, Uncle, and the list goes on. Someone is always watching and wondering how did you do it? My question to you is will you lead by example so that others can follow?

Great Quotes That Have Inspired Me

➢ "Carve you name on hearts, not tombstones. A legacy is etched into the mind of others and the stories they share about you."

Shannon L. Alder

➢ "If you would be forgotten as soon as you are dead, either write something worth reading or do something worth writing."

Benjamin Franklin

➢ "Languages allow us to reach out to people to touch them with our innermost fears, hopes, disappointments, and victories. To reach out to people, we will never meet. It is the greatest legacy your children and loved ones: The history of how you felt."

Simon Van Booy

➢ "Delight yourself in the Lord and He will give you the desires of your heart."

Psalm 37:4, the Word of God

Chapter Five
What Does Leadership Mean To Me?

When I think of leadership and what it means to me, it means responsibility to clear a path to create, inspire, reclassify, creating legacy everywhere. If you have a desire to be a leader, or currently are a leader, leadership should mean something to you.

Leadership should have value to you, as the leadership of others has led you added value to your life. I wouldn't have grown or achieved success if I did not have leaders to impart wisdom or correct me when I was working. Their help cultivated my gifts and talents and trained me in weak areas, or where I had no experience or knowledge at all. , Because of them, I strived for excellence in all that I placed my mind, heart and hands to do. The value of those leaders past and present, mean so much to me.

Currently, I am a General Manager for a multi-billion dollar corporation. Originally, I did not start in this role but started as a part-time cashier who worked mostly evenings and weekends. Some may call this the bottom of the barrel, but it was at the bottom that I knew there was a top and the height to that top was beyond what I ever could have imagined. God's word tells us in Ephesians 3:20 "Now to him who is able to do exceeding abundantly above all that we ask or think, according to the power that works in us."It is God's power that works in us that opens doors for us. Proverbs 18:16 says "that a man's gifts make room for him, and brings him before great men."

I recall in my career growth and various positions where God would place me in the presence those called the "Important" people, the "Big Wigs" or, the "Top Dogs." God allowed me to be in the right place at the right time. My being around these people was a regular occurrence. It was in those moments that God seemed to position me on the right path to allow my gifts and talents to make room for me. These leaders would see the potential in me and mentor me and guide me. Before I knew it, I was moving to the next level that was always beyond my imagination.

As I grew to a position of handling a $100 million dollar building, it took some time to understand completely the full depth of what God was doing in the natural. My natural experience was a release of preparation for the supernatural. I began to pray, kneel before and seek the Lord for more clarity. As I matured in my faith and grew in the things of God, I gained wisdom about my purpose in the season that He had me in. God also revealed and why He had me there. The Lord began to speak more to my spirit and said, the world could trust me to be a good steward of large capacities with increased responsibility. The experience and He would prepare me for the territory He had ordained for me; a territory that is greater than where I currently am and beyond what I could ever imagine. The Lord said I want you to look as far as you can see. When the Lord spoke to me Shaniequa, said, "Accept your platform of this position as preparation for greater works for God."

It was the critical moments that made me the leader I am. It was the toughest assignments that required the most endurance and trust that God is with me and the lamp unto my feet. There were times where I felt that there was nothing good to come from some of the tasks and the assignments given, I felt that the pressure and the crushing would break me. However, the true test was–my willingness to see it through instead of just throwing in the towel and walking away when the road became rough. The tough times taught me faithfulness, dependability and showed those who counted on me that I would see it through. I've also learned you never get to pick who God calls you to serve or minister. We have our cherry picking ministries where we state our case of who we're called to Minister to, but God will place you in a situation to stretch you beyond yourself and yield yourself to Him. The key is you have to listen and stay in sync with God, even in the workplace, even as a leader. Allow God to plant you, so you are deeply rooted in what He has called you to do. And this will bring stability to your faith and increased trust in the fact that He will finish what He has started in your life.

I recall early in leading being the "Moses" in the workplace. At the beginning of my leadership career, I vacillated between micro-managing everything and completely abdicating my role. After some time, frustration, burn out, and finally realizing that God's word says that He shall supply all of my needs. Also, my needs could not be met if I would not accept the gifts He has given me called help in the form of employees and supervisors. That's when I quickly learned delegation.

I often laughed at this portion of reading about Moses when the Bible talked about his staff. I learned that this was exactly what God supplied me with, staff that could get the job done. Not using the staff caused me to be overwhelmed in leadership as Moses was in Exodus 18. The joy of what I loved to do the most was going, but I knew that I loved most. I now know that I love to lead people to a place of their destiny, just as God did for me through people who saw the unique and peculiar in me. Upon the further revelation, I realized that your personal leadership has to lead you to your spiritual leadership. If you are doing it alone in the natural, it makes it hard to embrace what you are supposed to spiritually. It was time to find who I was as a leader according to God's word.

As Moses had some problems in leadership, he had his first leadership consultant, Jethro. I had to find my leadership consultant, my mentor. Mentorship is vitally important in leadership as you need someone to lead and guide you with a greater moral compass. I began to find mentors who led according to Godly principles, who lived a life according to their teaching, who guided in wisdom, and certainly, ones I could trust.

As I began my journey to leadership, my first mentor was God, even though I did not have the relationship to trust and understand God as I do today. It was the influential leaders who imparted wisdom and great teachings that have brought me to the place that I would do God's will. It was those leaders that pushed me to the place where I could begin to hear Gods voice for myself, I learned through them gleaning from the God in them how to get into Gods presence.

At the beginning of my leadership career, I was mirrored in the story of Moses in Exodus 18:13-16 when Moses led the Israelites out of Egypt. In the midst of the Sinai desert, Moses found himself laboring from early morning to late night attempting to resolve every issue and conflict that arose. In other words, I had become a workaholic just as Moses was. I recall being promoted to my first store that did not meet company expectations, nor did staff operate at the expected level. The leadership staff appointed to me was disengaged due to past issues that spilled over into the current. I labored day and night and tried to do it all. It was a divine intervention from God that brought me to my senses. I recognized all of the laboring in the world was not going to change anything if it was unsustainable and did not include direction and wisdom from God. Jethro, Moses' father-in-law, was a priest of Midian. He saw that Moses workload was not sustainable and that Moses was headed for destruction. It was those great mentors that saw when I was headed to a dead end road that intervened to help me to see what I was missing because I was too far in the weeds. Those leaders helped me see what was important and allowed me to regroup and create boundaries that would sustain me as an effective leader. Being in leadership is great, but when we are ineffective, what is the cost? I had to, as Moses did, admit that working non-stop is not sustainable.

As defined in Exodus 18:17-18, we must realize it is not effective to work 12 to 18 hour days or six and seven days a week and survive.

Something is going to break down in our faith, trust, sanity, family, health, or the people around us who cannot take us anymore. During the breakdown, you can be certain that you will barely be able to stand yourself and will eventually be lead to walk away from your destined purpose. Just admit it; your strategy may not be working!

In leadership, it is really important to understand your unique calling. Jethro saw that Moses had many talents but had a unique calling that added significant value alone. In Exodus 18:19-20 Jethro shared with Moses wise counsel. He told Moses that God would be with him and that he should stand before God for the people so that he could bring their difficulties to God. Moses, Jethro said, should teach the people God's statutes and the laws, and show them the way in which they must walk and the work they must do. You cannot do it all. There has to be a place of release.

The word of God teaches us to seek wise counsel from those mentors that live according to

God's word. They will impart wise counsel to lead us into a place of prosperity that will increase spiritual and personal growth. In leadership, it's impossible to be the cup and the pitcher. One person pours while one receives what is being poured. The pitcher is always higher than the cup. Therefore, you must be willing to get low to receive the outpouring.

In personal leadership it is really important to know where you add value- know what you are called to do and what you have been qualified to do. Understand in leadership you will not always have the ability to do everything to perfection as there are some things that were just not meant for you to do. When that happens, we can find value in other people's gifts and talents that may be utilized. In leadership, it is wise to understand you are no good as a leader if you are the only one who can do it. When you leave the work stops and when you return it is waiting for you where you left off that cannot work. A great leader is always willing to duplicate themselves and not threatened by others' gifts and talents. Jethro was very practical. He established an organizational hierarchy with a different level of responsibilities.

In today's world, this is equivalent to creating a team, in large organizations they have a leadership team. The team is spearheaded by senior leadership and directives are carried out and through multiple levels of management, in the military it is according to ranking. In church, the Pastor is unable to do it all, so he trains up a staff, a ministerial team, which is are equipped to continue to build the kingdom and edify God. The key is willingness to give others authority, understanding that mistakes will come, which is, the price to pay for leadership.

Learn to manage by exception. Jethro advocated that Moses manage this same way. Scripture teaches in Exodus 18:22, "And let them judge the people at all times. Every great matter they shall bring to you, but any small matter they shall decide themselves. So it will be easier for you, and they will bear the burden with you."

Jethro says two things here first that Moses will be able to endure, and second that the people will be at peace. In other words, Moses' strategy would be more sustainable, and there would be fewer conflicts. This teaching shows me that your personal leadership has to mean more to you than it means to others. Leader, how would people rate your leadership? If you have a desire to lead, how will you learn from the teachings using Biblical principles to guide you in leading?

Reflections:

> In this chapter, what stood out to you most?

> What does leadership mean to you?

> Do you have a mentor?

> What do you think about being a mentor to someone else?

Chapter Six
To Lead, You Must First Follow

To become a great leader, you must first follow the directions of leadership appointed to you in your time of learning, growth and development.

In this current generation, many find themselves struggling to follow the instructions of those chosen to lead them. One would say that they feel as if independence or freedom was robbed when in actuality it is the foundation of where their freedom and independence can be birthed. If you take careful thought as a leader, there are daily routines that must be implemented to accomplish the tasks that lay before you and to ensure that execution takes place flawlessly. If you are not willing to follow, how do you expect to lead those you desire to follow you? When asking yourself am I a good leader, one of the other things you must ask is, do I struggle to follow?

Do I know the true characteristics of a good leader?

Allow me share with you five characteristics of being a good leader and how these five key points can change the way you lead more effectively:

1. **Flexibility**: we must understand that everything does not always go as we plan it. When this happens, we have to stay the course and not be discouraged. Listen to the guidance that is being placed before you, seek wisdom in the right places and don't become so prudent that you are not able to change when necessary.

2. **Communication**: this is critically important as someone else has to know what is taking place other than you. Lack of communication leads to poor perception and perception eventually becomes a reality and what one may think of you. Know the line of communication which is effective. In this

age where technology is prevalent everyone does not function well in this arena. Some people are personable, and desire face to face communication so communicate well respect the avenue that will lead to the best level of communication. Know who you are communicating with, to, and what will capture their attention. Understand that communication is a two-way street and those involved in the communication are people who not only want to listen but have someone who responds back to them respectfully.

3. **Courage**: sometimes you may have to stand alone and be fine with that. In leading people, not everyone will get on the bus at the same time. There are times where there may be a pulling, and it may not be in the direction of your vision. However, you have to be the one who is willing to stand the watch even when it may mean standing alone.

4. **Humility**: people must be able to talk and communicate with their leaders without feeling intimidated or pressured. No one wants to work with Mr. or Mrs. Perfect where the only thing right is them. We must be transparent and open minded enough to realize that people are human too. Leading means that you often have to be tough, but should always be fair. People will respect that about you.

5. **Responsible**: people want to work for someone that they can trust to give and stand by their word, even when, they didn't make the right decision. Being responsible and transparent go hand in hand in leadership. If there is blame, you must be willing to accept for anything that it is on you. Ownership is critical in being an effective leader. Let's hit the part about accolades. Real leaders don't take all the credit believing it was all them. Even if the

vision came from you, there were people who helped to push it through.

When you begin to take a look at history, there are several parallel moments that show there is a foundation of leadership lead from these principals.

From the beginning of creation, it was established that instructions were commanded by God with an expectancy of them being followed. Let's take a close look at Adam and Eve in the Garden of Eden. God gave a clear, concise commandment that Adam was not to eat from the tree of knowledge. From this Adam was to lead the earth, follow the directions of God, and direct Eve to do the same. The serpent deceived Eve, and Adam had no knowledge of the conversation between Eve and the serpent. Adam failed to follow the direct commandments of God and from this we see the fall of man.

What does this demonstrate? If Adam had stood firm and followed the commands, he would have yielded to the direction of his leadership instead of being persuaded and misguided by what Eve did. She questioned her total belief in what God had established which impacted current and future generations. This impact is still alive even now as the word of God states in Genesis 3:13-19. "And the Lord God said to the women, "What is this you have done?" The women said, "The serpent deceived me, and I ate."

So the Lord God said to the serpent: "Because you have done this, you are cursed more than all cattle and more than every beast of the field; upon your belly you shall go, and you shall eat dust all the days of your life. And I will put enmity between you and the woman, And between your seed and her seed; He shall bruise your head, And you shall bruise his heel."

"To the woman he said: I will greatly multiply your sorrow in conception; in pain you shall bring forth a children; your desire shall be for your husband, And he shall rule over you."

Then to Adam he said, "Because you have heeded the voice of your wife, and have eaten from the tree of which I commanded you, saying, "You shall not eat of it: "Cursed is the ground for your sake; in toil you shall eat of it, all the days of your life. Both thorns and thistles shall bring it forth for you, And you shall eat the herb of the field. In the sweat of your face you shall eat bread, till you return from to the ground, for out of it you were taken; for dust you are, and to dust you shall return."

From this, we see that even though God has given us the free will of choice, His will is for us to follow the commandments that He has placed before us. In leadership, you will have the ability to make decisions, however, failing to follow the right decisions come with consequences. The part about this that is so detrimental is when those consequences based on your decision not only impact you, but those also connected to you. One of the things that God has commanded is that we have authority, leaders, over us. If we are to take an oath in being a great leader, then it behooves us to understand Romans 13:1-7. This scripture fully illustrates what God has established concerning leadership and us following the leaders that He has placed over us. Let's take a look:

> Romans 13:1 Let every person be subject to the governing of authorities. For there is no authority except God, and the authorities that exist are appointed by God.

> Romans 13:2 So the person who resists such authority resists the ordinance of God, and those who resist, bring judgment upon themselves.

> Romans 13:3 For rulers are not a terror to do good works but to evil. Do you want to be unafraid of the authority? Do what is good, and you will have praise from the same.

> Romans 13:4 For he is God's minister to you for good. But if you do evil, be afraid: for he does not bear the sword in vain; for he is God's minister, an avenger to execute wrath on him who practices evil.

> ➤ Romans 13:5 Therefore you must be a subject, not only because of wrath but also for conscience sake.

> ➤ Romans 13:6 For because of this you also pay taxes, for they are God's ministers continually to do this very thing.

> ➤ Romans 13:7 Render therefore to all their due: taxes to whom taxes are due, customs to whom customs, fear to whom fear, honor to whom honor.

Romans 13 cites as the biblical backing for the following concepts. Everyone should submit to those in authority over them whether it is a husband, pastor, employee or apostle. Everyone who is in authority is Gods delegated authority. Those who resist God's delegated authority are resisting God. We must keep in mind that God certainly ordained that we follow leadership. However, He did not command us to follow those who rebel against His commandments and the order which He has established. God wants us to be wise in our decisions. Gentle reminder that, in all God has established there are seasons for those things to come to pass (refer to Ecclesiastes for more insight). The bottom line is we must submit to something greater than ourselves to gain wisdom and knowledge to become greater leaders than those who have birthed greatness in us.

When I reflect on a great Biblical example of one who followed all of the instructions of God and was a faithful follower, I think of Joshua. He even followed the instructions when they seemed strange. At the beginning of his life, he was subject to things that we, in this day, would not be able to handle. He was an Egyptian slave working under cruel task masters, but because of his obedience, he rose to be the leader of Israel. Joshua obediently followed the strange instructions of God for the battle of Jericho. For six days, the army marched around the city. On the 7th day (time), they marched, shouted, and the walls fell flat. We sometimes think the things our leaders ask us to do are vague, have no value, and will serve no purpose or do no good. Sometimes it is the simplest task that will give us the greatest reward. Joshua learned a lot as a student while serving under Moses' leadership. He showed great courage despite the huge responsibility assigned to him. How do we handle the responsibility assigned to us and how invested and committed are we to the things entrusted to us? We are commanded to follow those whom God has appointed over us to lead and guide us, and we have to be great students as we learn from the life of Joshua. We must live a life of obedience and from that we will receive great rewards from God.

Take a moment to reflect. If you are a leader or have a desire to lead, do you have an issue with authority and submitting to what has been established? If so, this will be a great command from God to follow on the road to being a "Great Leader" appointed and established by God. You decide. How will you lead?

Chapter Seven

Leading Through the Three P's
Purpose, Personal, Passion

As a leader, your authority should always serve a purpose and have a personal impact through the passion. This passion should reside within you to press through all obstacles, trials, and adversity that may come your way. The definition of the word purpose is the reason for which something is done or created or for which something exists. As a verb, it is defined as, one's intention or objective. Many times, as our lives face difficult challenges and obstacles, we tend to define ourselves as having no purpose. We find ourselves measuring our worth based on how well life is going. Many will define their purpose in their lives and their personal sense of fulfillment. I guess this is considered, what I will call, independence. Those that define their places of purpose define the meaning of good, of bad and will align to what one may think is right in one's own eyes.

In my life, I have had some trials and tribulations, but one would look at me and never think the testimony I give is a picture of what they thought my life would have been. I grew up for the most of my life in the city areas of New York. I lived in Queens during the early part of my youth and spent most of my teen years in the Bronx. I had parents who did do a great job of teaching morals, standards, and respect but did not always live according to the teachings they gave. There was a period when my parents had an addiction to drugs and alcohol. During these trying times as a child, I lived in a state of always wondering, "Why am I here and why did my parents bring me into this world to do this to me?" For much of my teen years and even into my early adult years, I lived with anger, resentment and felt as if was not worth it to do anything great. I grew up with confidence issues and had no sense of security in who I was. With the challenges and the difficulty of forgiving my parents and finding worth for myself, I began to rebel. I had a mindset of finding what made me happy and created my personal purpose.

I recall going to nursing school and becoming New York State Certified. Although I became certified, I was not able to stay on this course because this was not the plan or the purpose that God had designed for my life. It was in my early twenties that a portion of the healing began. I started to get more connected to God but was not totally sold out to God. But, God is gracious and merciful? At this time, things began to transition in my life, and I would find myself in church with a desire to lead and wanting to help to do the work of the God. However, I still had struggles with being transparent, as I was ashamed of whom I was and the life I had to live to become the person God ordained me to be. When I was 19, I lost my dad to a massive heart attack and found myself struggling again saying,

"God, why is this happening to me? As soon as I began to forgive and build a relationship with him, you take him from me." A huge void in my heart and my life began because as a child I so longed for the daddy and daughter conversations. Just as soon as they began, they quickly ended. I had bitterness within me, and would find myself hurting people because of my personal hurt.

The one I would afflict most often was my mother. A wedge was created in our relationship as I held her hostage to her past and tried to make her pay forward for her past mistakes. In the year of 2004 - 2005 a real transition took place. One thing I always prayed for was the total deliverance for my mom not realizing that God had a purpose for my life, as well. At that time, I began to grow stronger in the Lord, and as I increased in my relationship with Him, He increased my capacity for the purpose He designed for me. I was operating in leadership over the youth and the ladies' auxiliary club. In 2006, my life was totally changed, and I began to see the God-given purpose for my life. I recall that year as if it was yesterday. I sat at the back of the church during a revival service, and a visiting Prophet called me up to pray for me. She, spot on, confirmed everything I was feeling, the hurt, the pain, the disappointment, resentment, and anger. She declared that it was for my good and that my life would be one of greatness. She also said that God was calling me to leadership to help build the kingdom. In this same year, I was groomed for a leadership position as Store Manager for a large corporation. At this time, my thought was that God called me to leadership for the corporate arena. However, the position I attained as a Store Manager was the greater. I truly believed one extent of the plan because I lacked understanding that there was a greater purpose ordained by God. As I began to draw closer to Him, I was able to see and understand His purpose for my life.

In 2008, I joined a church, Love House Ministries, under the leadership of Pastor Randy & Theresa Roberts. It was then that my life completely unfolded, and the true provision for what God had established for my life began to be clear. I got a double portion of blessings. Not only did God give me exactly what I needed in the way of great leaders who have a heart after God, but He also gave me the greatest spiritual parents that I could ever dream of having. Pastor Randy filled that void for the daddy-daughter conversations I longed for which brought healing and peace in my life. Love House Ministries is where I experienced the true deliverance of God, and total healing took place. I repented before God for the hurt and anguish I caused my mom. I faced her, apologizing, for holding her in bondage to what the enemy told her she was, even though God had a totally different plan for her life.

See, her addiction to drugs and alcohol served a purpose under God. She now ministers to those who suffer from addiction issues and helps them to find healing, deliverance and devote their lives to Christ. It was not until I was delivered and set free from my hurt, I was able to acknowledge the great call that God had for my mom. I understood why her trials were necessary for my life in equipping me for who God called me to be. It was seeing the greatness of God's transforming power, something that man could never do, that caused me to become a "sell out" for God!

I will never forget that day when I received the email from my Pastor in 2011 that stated "If you are receiving this letter it is because you are selected for ordination. Please respond if you will accept the call of God." I cried for hours. I remember turning the computer off and on several times and reading the email over and over again and saying to God, "Lord you saw fit for me to lead in your kingdom? Lord, you trust me enough to be able to stand before your people?" Even after I accepted the call, growth had to take place to find exactly where God wanted me to be. As I matured in God's word and the things of God, I found my total purpose was first to glorify Him! As you live to glorify God, the visions that He will birth in you will begin to come. I always had a great desire to teach about leadership and to create an atmosphere where God can step in, and activation takes place. I have a great passion to work with the youth and am purposed to work with women in ministry. My call is to teach them how to live a righteous life and uphold the standards that God has ordained with no compromise while still having fun. Who says being a Christian has to be boring?!?!?! God's word declared that we were created to glorify Him, to proclaim His greatness, and to accomplish His will. It was not until I finally said, "Not my will Lord, but thy will be done in my life," I could see the worth I held. I also saw how important I was to God, and His master plan. Today I say, "To God be the Glory, and I live to serve you totally Lord and walk with the purpose of helping your children to know more about you and your goodness."

In leading through the three P's, the personal is truly important. How can you lead or teach something you don't know. It has to be personal to be real. People seek a personal connection to those who lead them, those who have wisdom based on personal experience and those who have overcome adversities. Your personal experiences help in fulfilling your purpose. If your life were filled with blank spaces, there would be no value to add to your purpose. Passion must have a connection to your purpose.

As I think of passion, I think of Christ, and His never-ending passion for doing the will of the Lord no matter the cost. Christ was tried, tested, accused, beaten, denied, and need I say more. However, His passion was only to seek the Father's will with all of His being and to be what God called Him to be. In leading through the three P's, we should lead in a way that shows such passion those connected to us will have such desire to lead with the same, and even more, passion. From Christ's passion, we should learn that as we lead we are going to be accused, tested and tried. However, we must lead from a place of integrity and personally choose to lead from a place of maturity and dignity.

Passion requires us to have a strong feeling or sense of what we do. Passion creates a portal by which to pursue your dreams and lead others to grab hold of their dreams and see them through. Passion requires a fight, even when it does not look like things are going well. When I think of passion, I think of it as the gas needed in the vehicle to get you where you need to go. I can have the vehicle and a destination, but without the gas I remain in the same position. When I correlate that in the perspective of our faith as a leader, when people see you they should see that you have a God. Your vehicle and your faith are your gas that lead you to a destination of living a righteous life of no compromise. When people seek leaders to follow, they seek those with integrity, morals and who exemplify the things they teach. Your purpose, your personal, and your passion will help people to see and understand who you are, what you're made of, and what you are willing to do.

**Chapter Eight**
The Gift That Keeps On Giving

Have you even been given a gift that had so much purpose you have used it more than you ever imagined you would? I recall being the gift of opportunity. There were those who saw the potential in me far beyond what I ever imagined and gave me a chance. They gave me the gift that kept on giving. It gave me the opportunity and access to success, and I have the ability to give someone this gift. When I reflect on this, it takes me to the biblical character of Abraham and how he had to leave all that was familiar to go to an unknown place. He had to trust firmly that God would have provision made for him because of his obedience

I remember the time when I was asked to move my entire family to an unfamiliar place called Beaufort, South Carolina. I had no family, no friends and had to trust that God would make provision for me. In Beaufort, I found who I was and what purpose God had for my life. God had to take me through all those experiences to be the remnant that would break generational curses. I was the first in my immediate family to rise from a lifestyle of living from paycheck to paycheck. I confessed Christ, became saved, and accepted the call to the leadership of Gods people. I now operate in high-level management. I found this portion of my destiny by willing to be planted; I found a church home that poured so much into me. That was the turning point for my personal and spiritual life, as it was here that I learned to trust God, totally. I truly accepted the gift of redemption and was given the ability to overcome; I am grateful I can now give a gift and pay it forward. This gift of life began here where I found who I truly was, and I am now able to walk in my purpose and give the gift that keeps on giving, the gift of God's love. When I think of the gift that God has given me that keeps on giving, it is the gift of helping. I love to help people reach their full potential. I am not always looking to be a winner but how I can help them win and achieve by this we all win.

I recall in my first Senior Leadership position receiving this young man who came to work for me. He felt he knew everything because he came from a high traffic area and thought because we were in the country that he had some things to teach us. This young man thought he "arrived" and ensured on a daily basis that he would find a way to prove himself as being better than everyone else. As time went on, he began to struggle to the point where his career was slipping through his fingers. I felt compelled to help this gentleman by leading and showing him how he could become an effective leader. While giving him the gifts called access it took some time and continued reinforcement, as some may not totally accept the gift, or accept it and find no purpose in the gift until an appointed time. Have you ever been given a gift that you liked but could not find the use of it at that moment? Have you ever put it away where it would still be in great condition for use at the right moment? Well, this is what this young man did, he did not totally reject the gift but at the time he did not see the need for the gift. There were times where I had to allow him to struggle alone to open his eyes to see there was no I in the team. He had to learn that in everything we struggle to do, there is someone whose done it before we thought to do it and completed it before we even attempted to try it. It was a journey of growing pains and building trust that I had his best interest at heart and by the testing he should show himself approved. With honor, I can say that I couldn't be prouder of this gentleman, Erik McCoy is his name. He has went far beyond what I could ever imagined, and he has adopted great concepts in his leadership and has developed great people as he received the gift that kept on giving. When it is effective, it will never stop affecting!

I will forever serve God and live to love people to life! This gift is immeasurable in that as you give, it has such value that it never devalues, and the pureness of its impact it spreads like wildfire. As you give more of it the value increases as it brings people into a new place of being. The gift that keeps giving doesn't end. It gives those who were lost the ability to see their way past common; it gives them the ability to hear beyond the sound of failure and know that they can do all things through Christ. It gives the ability to do; as God will do above all they can ask or think in their lives. It gives them the ability to speak of the goodness of the Lord and how the provision made for the gift of His love allowed them to overcome. My life, gives me the ability to impact someone else's life! Take the time to reflect on how you can do this as a leader, or if you have a desire to lead, how you can become that leader that continues to give the gift that gives more.

As I think of people who continue to have a powerful impact on people's lives because of the gift they gave, I remember Dr. Martin Luther King, Jr. What I learned from Dr. King is that all he started was with the love of Christ, and through this he gave the gift of love for people and equality for all people. That gift still spreads and makes provision for many all around the world. Dr. King had a purpose, and his passion was driven by a personal desire to see people treated fairly. He led from the front and spoke God's word to the people. He stood firm on the fact that no matter how bad he was treated or ridiculed for what he was doing he would do the will of God for his life. While teaching those fundamentals of living a righteous life, Dr. King gave many gifts. He gave knowledge to those who did not know, and he gave others vision to see what could never be imagined. He allowed many to see what could happen if you will seek first the kingdom of God and His righteousness. Matthew 6:33 goes on to say that as you "seek Christ first that all of these things shall be added unto you", that is gifts and abilities. The result of Dr. King doing what God called him to do, unafraid, was desegregation, equality, and justice for all.

What gift has God equipped you with to edify and build the kingdom? Have you a gift to lead people into a place of prosperity while giving them the tools to get to a place of obedience to God and walk out their destiny? Imagine if you'd never met the people that God created to teach you, guide you and lead you, or if you had not accepted the gifts of knowledge, direction, and wisdom. Would you count your life to be the same? I can't speak for you, but I can certainly speak for me and say that my life would not have been the same! There are things that I have seen that I would never have looked for. There are places I have been that I would have never desired to go. There are people who I have connected to that I never imagined and there is the source, my heavenly Father, that is my strength that I never imagined would be my all! Thank you, Lord, for the gift of your love that leads your people to a place of purpose.

This particular chapter requires a moment of reflection to understand the "who" and the "what". Take a moment to think of those significant moments in your life that you may have just called it luck, but was a gift that kept on giving. You may still be reaping the benefits of that gift today. Write these things down in the space provided.

_____

_____

_____

_____

_____

_____

_____

_____

_____

_____

Now as we reflect on these gifts that we have received let's take the time to give back! Share the wealth and give the gift of knowledge. Be the leader who will give those tools (gifts) to place in the toolbox for when the time comes, those individuals who follow are ready to go to work!

Chapter Nine
Your Legacy Should Always Be Greater Than You

Many, who lead, do so to a certain degree and then stop. This style of leadership is capped, or shall I say, preserves the ability to remain in control without the underlying fear of being replaced. When you look at this, I would ask, "Would it make sense to fear being replaced?" Guess what? Replacement is inevitable, unless you have the ability to live forever! Great leaders take great joy in birthing and investing in those that will become greater than them, as things will go farther than they can take it in their time of leadership. This behavior, is not a sign of a poor or weak leader but a sign of a wise leader. The person who can see beyond themselves and understand that in order for there to be a legacy of greatness, someone else must become greater.

The definition of legacy is a gift or bequest, which is handed down, endowed or conveyed from one person to another. It is something that is transmitted, inherited or received from a predecessor. Legacy is more about sharing what you have learned; it gives a view of your life from a generational perspective. When I think of a true example of legacy, I think of the biblical character Elisha, who was Elijah's successor. Elisha was the faithful disciple of the prophet Elijah. Elisha followed his master from the moment they met. When Elijah disappeared in a fiery chariot up to heaven, Elisha cried out, "My father, my father the chariot of Israel". It was then Elisha knew he had a great work to do in carrying the mantle of Elijah in spreading the knowledge of God. Elisha felt from within, the spirit of Elijah. When you follow those that have led from a great place, you can feel their spirit as you come to know who they are. You can then lead from a place of integrity and honor.

As a leader, you will have greatness connected to you, and should never be threatened or worried that your replacement is operating better than you. It should be your desire; they can receive and carry the mantle to continue the legacy of greatness. Also, have the desire to raise up a great standard so that those who have gleaned from you can produce more fruit, take the torch, and go further. This teaches and molds true greatness!

If you are a parent, as you instill the things of your heart into your children, your desire is that they would do far better than you have done and become more successful than you were. You present great examples and teachings to guide them to become leaders and not followers. As a leader, you should have the desire to empower your teams and lead them to a place of operating at a greater level than you. I always say the true example of leadership is not when you are present, but when you are not present. Your absence will reflect what you have instilled in your people as they are a reflection of your teachings. When an outsider can look inside and not tell the difference except who is standing before them, that means there were great teachings from a great leader who understood that their role and responsibility was to raise the standard for others to be greater.

In the course of being a leader and training up greatness, there may be times when there is an idea that you had never thought of or a tactic that may work better. Don't become threatened by a working brain! As a leader, I seek those who can lead and are not glorified task masters that only pile up lists for completion without any ground for the purpose behind what they say they master at doing. It is great that they can meet deadlines, but if issues arise in your absence they are bound to fail at making a decision because they weren't molded to become a leader the moment you need them to be one. I once heard a cliché in the corporate world which said, "Some of the most successful leaders are the lazy ones." That means they have to teach everything because they never want to do anything. Now don't get me wrong. I would never imply that you be a lazy leader. Nobody wants to produce laziness. But I will say that if you are the only one that knows, get ready to be the only one who does it all! Trust is a huge factor in passing the torch, and this comes with faithfulness. When one is faithful in the small things, they can be trusted with those larger assignments. As a leader, create those opportunities where those you lead can show if they are faithful and as this is proven, mold away! Let's just settle this. God saw fit for Jesus without worrying that he was going to overthrow Him. A good leader will mold a great leader, a leader that will follow the vision.

Now let's self-reflect. Have you led those who you have felt, "Hum...are they going to take my place?" Well, how do you become greater and move into your new place of destiny if you only invest and develop you? Let's deal with the issues that prevent you from letting go. Time to talk about it! Take a moment and write down a couple of things that seem to prevent you from totally releasing and trusting those who you have lead, see greatness in, but just won't let go.

_____

_____

_____

_____

_____

_____

_____

"Leadership reveals itself in the big moments, but it is forged in the small. It is the exponential and compounding product of our many incremental behaviors and actions; all of which arise out of our choices in values, beliefs and emotions. Choices all. Not one is thrust upon us."

--Christopher Babson

Chapter Ten
When Leadership Is Ineffective

What happens in leadership when what you have been doing for years does not impact what it used to or produce what it used to produce? Does it seem that you can't move ahead or have become stagnant in your performance and ability to execute at a high level? Do you feel like you are stuck? It's time to shift! Often in leadership as things change in the atmosphere and things require something different to impact differently we often have to do a paradigm shift to remain effective and impactful. In leadership adopting change can seem hard especially when you have operated in the same rhythm and routine. Doing this has worked for you for the majority of your career and led you to the place of success but won't seem to take you beyond that success to a greater level.

In looking at what creates that halt in leadership, one of those aspects come from failing to create better leaders that come in with fresh ideas and can easily identify what has become common tasks versus purpose. They can see what produces nothing because all it produces is a check in the task box. New talent and a fresh eye can give you the ability to see with a new lens. There are often in the common practice of routine that we see the same thing day in and day out that we didn't even recognize when it took a turn.

A good leader is always being developed and molded, so in turn they develop and mold those they have the responsibility to nurture and develop. The importance of recognizing when there is no impact in producing good fruit has to be an immediate discerning of what is creating this ineffectiveness and weeding out these ineffective inadequacies immediately. If not, the familiarity of poor traits will begin to spread massively. There are five key essential ways to do a self-check and identify have I become an ineffective leader, or is someone under the hierarchy or leadership connected to my success become ineffective.

1. **Poor Character**: A leader who lacks character or integrity will not endure. They may have the highest of intelligence, great wisdom, and even be savvy at what they do. If you see signs of them trying to rationalize unethical behavior with no ownership or personal remorse they will eventually fall prey to their undoing.

2. **Poor Communication Skills**: They find a list of excuses in why they could not tell you or they place the blame of delegated messages upon someone else. Pay attention to the common excuse of "I truly thought you knew". It becomes even more detrimental when they refuse to accept the fact that they failed to communicate and in that the overall impact that goes beyond themselves.

3. **Self-Serving Nature**: When a leader fails to recognize or understand the concept

of "service above self" In this you will find tons of arrogance, pride and a vote of no-confidence from their subordinates.

4. **Not a Forward Thinker**: Satisfied with the status quo, not recognizing inconsistencies and moments of decline in performance or results. One who has a mindset of survival than rather than persistence or growth. No vision equals no leadership.

5. **Not Accountable**: Leaders who do not reflect and ask how I played a part in what just happened. It is never my fault. The one who refuses to be accountable will claim all of the credit for praise and acceptance but place blame where there is no solution or resolve to an identified issue.

When this behavior is noticed, it is imperative that it is addressed. If this is you, then it's very important to seek the mentorship of one who will be biased and critical in criticism. You need a mentor that will give you what you need and not what you want. Ask yourself or look at others and find if they are being traditional or following religious practices that don't provide long term results that would be passed on. In the Bible in the book of Haggai we can see ineffective leadership, where there was incompetency, laziness, and neglect these are the same issues we often face. However in Haggai we can clearly see how God has to address these issues and clearly show what He wanted to be done and how He wanted it done. God pinpointed the issues and focused on the people and why things were not getting done to the root of the issues. In leadership the only way we can remain effective is to understand the underlying issues of poor communication. There is also, lack of teamwork, ineffective direction, the list can go on, however as the leader you must be in tune with what is the impact and must begin to reconstruct! How do we reconstruct or how do we turn this around are the questions we should be asking in those times of the latter.

The first key to this is personal ownership and being vested. To gain that effectiveness back again, you must understand the root of your error and then begin to plan and understand what you seek to be the result. You must understand this before you start, or you will never have a measurable goal or even recognize if what you're asking for is sustainable.

In moving forward, you must have zeal and kill the spirit of procrastination. Successful people don't wait when they know what they are supposed to be doing or achieving. Embrace those failures and constantly look back at those pitfalls and test the current to see if the trend is on the same path or if it is moving in the right direction. Be honest with yourself know when you need to seek wise counsel if this is a road of the unfamiliar. Be wise not to walk in blindly.

Understand the pace of the goal and don't get to far ahead of yourself that you are unable to determine if a mistake occurred. Also make sure you spend so much time trying to go back and fix what should have been established. Stay on course and be consistent even when it gets tough. It is easy to quit but when you re-commit it is not as easy to find yourself in the place where you need to be because you will have to catch up.

One of my favorite scriptures speaks to me daily is Romans 12:2 "And be not transformed: but be ye transformed by the renewing of your mind, that ye may prove what is that good, acceptable, and perfect will of God." When you renew your mind God will test you, and you will have the ability to discern if you are in right standing. Renewal is critical in leadership as we will consistently be tested to see if we understand what happened, why it needed to happen and can we handle it. Can we be trusted? These are some ways we will know if we are in the right place in leadership. Most leaders will recognize when they have turned off the path and know when a dead end road is ahead. It's not the leader who can see it that is the best leader but the one who recognizes it, steps out, does something to intervene, prevents destruction. What happens when you have to be the only one to stand and take the charge? It is not always easy, but it is necessary and is a part of the call of being an effective leader. Right now in leadership over our nation and in Christianity we can clearly see the impact of inconsistency and not training up the next generation to do greater exploits than we could ever do. We see the moral compass bastardized and no reverence to the established foundation of this Country. We hear the words "In God We Trust", or "God Bless America" but see so much double standard and inconsistency in how we lead, how we react, that its created a portal of lack of trust for one another and what we stood for. This generation questions, is there truly an "American Dream"? We can't afford not to take heed to understanding what is required to become an effective leader. If we find that our leadership has become ineffective, we have to use constantly, the compass that God has given us called the Bible to lead us and guide us into all truth. We have to seek those leaders that understand when to shift, have shifted, and steadily climbed to sustained greatness in what they have been called to do. Jeremiah 17:7-8 "Blessed is the man who trusts in the Lord. He is like a tree planted by the water, that sends out its roots by the stream, does not fear when heat comes, for its leaves remain green, and is not anxious in the year of drought, for it does not cease to bear fruit."

Reflections:

1. Do you find yourself thinking only about you and do not understand what it means to provide servant leadership? Yes or No?

2. Do you make constant excuses and find yourself trying to wiggle out of situations? Yes or No?

3. Have you lowered your morals and in turn your team has followed your lead? Yes or No?

Chapter Eleven
The Truth Of The Matter!

In leadership, the great one's always make leading look so easy. Great leaders have the ability to wear many hats and do it with such charisma that you will say to yourself, "Well if they can do it, guess what, I can do it too." It is true! You can do it! However, we don't know the cost to get where they are. Great leaders have been inspired and trained up by other great leaders who gave them the ability to multitask and to be impactful and purposeful. However, we often miss the key point that they were trained up, inspired by greatness and worked hard. We often want the success without the works.

I recall a point in my life where I concentrated my Bible study on "faith without works is dead" in James 2:14-26. During this study, I saw that in certain areas of my life I had great faith and believed that God would do it. However, there were things God required of me that went beyond just my prayers and required some work on my behalf. It wasn't until I did the work that these things came to pass. If you desire to be a great leader, you must realize that it is more than sitting and watching. You have to be in the trenches. The Word teaches us that to whom much is given much is required (Luke 12:48). We often want more, but we are not willing to do more as required to receive more. Great leaders are devoted and faithful in their good doings which often means sacrifice and being uncomfortable. It's not always fun and sometimes the benefits are not immediate. It may require you stay in a position until God sees fit for you to move. The question is, "Are you willing?" The rubber meets the road when one acquires the position but not willing to do the extra things that may be needed by them. It is very easy as a boss to say, "GO", but true leaders often say, "Let's go!" It is not always easy when half of those you are calling to go with you are out of sync. Sometimes, as a leader, you constantly have to recalibrate the team and reset the boundaries to get everyone on the same playing field. These necessary actions can cause delays in the success process. At this point staying the course may become rough, tiresome and require more than you think you are capable of actually giving. Being an effective leader means that when everyone gives up you have no choice but to keep moving and seek, along the way, like-minded individuals who can grab a hold of and help to push the vision. Being that great leader means that even when you are discouraged you still have to encourage. If there is the sound of bitterness, complaining, and murmuring be prepared to receive those poor achievements! Being that great leader means you often have to put in what nobody else is willing to put in and being okay. Know that you are operating in purpose to equip and produce more.

I worked for a leader once who said, "The conductor has to conduct even if the symbols fall. Then they must get the harp or the violin to pick up the sound to offset the difference so that nobody would ever know the difference." A leader (conductor) must continue to conduct business when nobody else thinks of the business, invests in, shows up for, knows how to, or when nobody even cares about the business. Think of how one could care less about your relationship with the Father. However, you still have to be a citizen of the kingdom and respond as a citizen of the kingdom when nobody values or respects citizens of the kingdom.

Leadership is a great calling and one of great fulfillment to see how God can use you to take a group of individuals to a place called success. Fear is the foothold to lack of success. It is a great barrier in the natural and a destroyer in the supernatural. It creates apprehension in one's ability to move in timing. Things will happen but often come in a reactive position instead of a proactive position that creates gaps of consistency and balance, causing confusion and chaos. We all know that God is a God of order.

As leaders, we have to ensure that we create balance and establish a protocol. Scripture states "Write the vision and make it plain" (Habakkuk 2:2). If we as leaders are operating in a "fly by the seat of our pants position", not knowing the plans from one minute to the next, our people lose the ability to find stability and trust causing them to be unstable in their doings. In other words, being a leader requires much from us. That is why the Bible declares that many are called, but few are chosen (Matthew 22:14). Many will step forward, but there are only a few chosen people to lead. Understand where you are, know what's required of you, and be willing to walk in the plans and the purpose of what God has established. Don't let your rubber meet the road and spin completely off the road.

As a leader, always invest in yourself. You cannot give someone something you do not possess. As a leader, "Write the vision and make it plain". Bumps come up on the road, but stay the course and do not detour. As a leader, be able to endure and never allow your emotions to lead. You must always inspire even while trying to inspire yourself. Most importantly, you must believe. You cannot expect your people to believe in what you are struggling to believe. There are so many more things to do as a leader, but the most important is to know first what and where has God called you to lead?

Take the time to reflect. How sure are you after reading all of these chapters that leadership is the place where God has called you to be?

_____

_____

_____

_____

_____

In leadership there are many things that inspire, teach and guide you to become a great leader. The key factor, of the listed, is the acceptance of what is provided as a tool to develop and mold you into greatness. Many things in our life we do not accept at the time as being a building block, however, there has to be an understanding and a continuance to step up to the place where God has destined for us to be. Many times we fight against the voice inside that speaks to us as we go through the highs and lows that lead us to the right spot in our lives. In leading, I learned one thing for sure I don't know everything and everything I gained was by the willingness to be taught that I may teach someone else. That's why God told us in Genesis 12:2 "I will make you into a great nation, and I will bless you; I will make your name great, and you will be a blessing" As we go on this journey, and become elevated we should rejoice in our blessings as well as take someone else to a place of elevation to be blessed. There will be times on this journey when it will be hard to face your past, to face your hurts that make you face yourself to be able to face your future. I say to you embrace; know that it will all work together for your good. When I think of life's bad moments, I think about that nasty medicine you receive when sick, it surely does not taste good at the time, but it really does make everything much better once digested! Digest what has happened, so that you can enjoy what can and will happen as long as you yield to what is happening. I must say this, don't be selfish, a selfish man dies alone, and never enjoys the full greatness of what it could be because he never allowed himself to see past himself. As you prevail and enter into that place of destiny, be real, stay true and never conform. Don't try to be something you are not, and cannot sustain. Why? Because it is not a part of who you're created to be.

My prayer is that this book has inspired you and opened a portal for you to position yourself as a mighty leader for the kingdom. In this walk, as a leader, we have more at stake than just financial posture. Lead as you desire to be led and according to our ordained manual of leadership, the Word of God!

Conclusion

As you have read this book, you can see that leadership is recognized as a complex enterprise and can be proven that effective leaders are more than just managers. In each chapter, it is clearly noted what can take place when ineffective leadership is on the scene. There are several elements that can be impacted such as character, morals, integrity, self-confidence and trust, to name a few. However effective and transformational leadership starts with you which as outlined in chapter five through seven, and it becomes a gift that will continue to give. Understand that where you came from or have been through is only an instrument to build effective character. Remember, you can never lead from where you've never been. As you receive the gift by following an exceptional leader, you are now molded and transformed into a great leader, which can give the gift to someone else to create a better leader!

God did call us to do greater work than He did. As we live today in a world that is living by its own rules and creating its own mantle of leadership, we can see that we are producing leaders who are not committed, selfish, lack ambition. Many leaders operate in a state of dominance. Take these few key things in closing and write them upon your heart. As a leader, there is a responsibility to lead people to a place of greatness and not a place of destruction. Ensure that you understand where you are, and you grasp when your leadership has become ineffective; note when you need to reposition your feet and move quickly. Always note that a good leader always carries these few characteristics of:

1. being flexible it can't be your way or the highway;

2. ability to communicate; people should be able to talk with you with no fear of retaliation;

3. having courage, sometimes tough decisions have to made, and tough conversations have to happen, people can sense humility;

4. not being the know it all, arrogance creates division, and finally;

5. being responsible; own your business, own your behavior and remember to take ownership when it is bad as much as you do when it is good.

Leadership is a great honorable place to be. However, it can do one of two things which is make good people or break good people. Stand firm on the foundation in which we were created, the Holy Bible. The good book is our guide to all things in life including leadership. I say to all leaders or those who have a desire to be a great leader, on which side do you stand? As a leader will you affect or infect?